ANCHORESS

ANCHORESS

A POEM

ESTA SPALDING

Published in 1997 by
House of Anansi Press Limited
1800 Steeles Avenue West, Concord, ON
Canada L4K 2P3

Distributed in Canada by
General Distribution Services Inc.
30 Lesmill Road
Toronto, Canada M3B 2T6
Tel. (416) 445-3333
Fax (416) 445-5967
e-mail: Customer.Service@ccmailgw.genpub.com

01 00 99 98 97   1 2 3 4 5

Canadian Cataloguing in Publication Data
Spalding, Esta
Anchoress
Poem.
ISBN 0-88784-591-6
I. Title.
PS8587.P214A8 1997   C811'.54   C97-930112-2
PR9199.3.S62A8 1997

Cover design: Pekoe Jones
Printed and bound in Canada
Typesetting: ECW Type & Art, Oakville

House of Anansi Press gratefully acknowledges the support
of the Canada Council and the Ontario Arts Council in
the development of writing and publishing in Canada.

for Kristin, Jane, and Douglas

Last night I found the red book the world lost,
the one which contains the address of the rain,
all the names of the beloved dead, and how
and where they can be reached.

> — *Li-Young Lee*

Where is my country, someone asks in sleep.

> — *Adam Zagajewski*

LAB NOTE
VANCOUVER AQUARIUM

January 17, 1992
Before Dawn

*Helen, I'm drowning. If I lie down in darkness will you
come, if I lie down in rain will you rescue me, arrive with
torches to dry my skin, tell me again the things that mattered?
Across the table, the candle brightening your face, how I looked
to you, sad, you said, your hands on my hands, I want to argue
with you again, hear you say, I have that bone to pick with
you, love or politics or too many spices in your arms till
morning.*

*What you loved was that I was Canadian, what you hated
was that I had no politics, someone owns your body, you said.*

You do, Helen.

Our own NAFTA I signed petitions against it.

How we laughed.

*Let's start over. Forget the whale, the aquarium, forget the
tagged bones, shipwrecked on the laboratory table. Melted,
France said, not human.*

*I could name the stars with you Helen Helen Helen Helen
though you hated science — you have to believe, take your
glasses off — there were code words in our language, cakes,
bloobs, yogs, night flight, oroboros, you left those — careless,
a pile of rags in your arms.*

*I polish the whale's bones, scrub with steel wool dipped in
bleach. You are not really gone until my skull is empty, those
pictures, mines you buried: your mother born into the cave,
your father diving into quarries, I dream again, again, your
parents falling like twin flames — you whispered that story
— France on her blue bicycle, how we swam naked in Lake
Michigan, water a shared garment, an unspooled turban, you
and France together in your kitchen telling your childhood as
if it were one story. You left her too, remember, terrorist. She
was halved without you. Just like you to get the last word in
— Peter, this is my war — then you vanished into leaf,
thumbprints of rain, into a smoke tree, charred city, Baghdad.*

Look at me, a half-man who can't sleep, who doesn't own his dreams, who lives with the manure stink beetles leave. A man crouched over his lover's grave, his hair in his face — mouth on your scalloped hip. I want you inside me, a second, deeper skin, my anchoress.

Helen, one year of drowning. Seeking you where you are hiding, I crawl into a beast.

One part of this is rage, I was your creature and abandoned.

ORIGINS

Stories told to me by Helen and France

                    In a cave
so dark they touch to see,
Manon is born.

Beside the Dordogne River, smell
of fresh water seeps
through dust into the narrow
slit in the cliff
behind the neighbour's house.
We climb here when we can.
Movement is dangerous.
Through the last months of the occupation
the neighbours carry bread, a bowl with whatever
water is not lost to the hillside,
they bring fruit, mashed for the baby
who cannot see the bright colour,
can only taste vividness.

Manon does not learn to use
her eyes — so little light.
(Every light is a risk
for you. For us.)

Paintings fifteen thousand years old, animals
in every pose
mobile, floating over her crib.

Though it isn't possible, her eyes
shut all those months, Manon
remembered the paintings,
told Helen and France about the bison,
reindeer, horse, ibex
limned onto the cave's side
in ochre stirred with saliva
sometimes painted, sometimes sprayed

by the human mouth,
or a thin tube like a whistle.
(The whole artist's tribe jointly laboured,
jointly imagined, visions mingling
in chalk-dust, red as dried blood,
brown as the earth of hills.
They gathered round a single wick burning
in hollowed stone, walnut oil.)

Manon's blank eyes, the colour won't blossom
in them without light. A rag
stuffed in her mouth to stop her cries.
Her only language: milk, the bright
sweetness of fruit.

Their father, Will
Indiana, 1962

Will ascribes to the corrosive diplomacy
of water: harder
than granite in the quarry
where his father is a boss,
but softer too,
                        cooling the metal saws
that cut the stone's shoulders —
rainwater, a bluer
blood, filling the machine-square holes
gouged in earth.

(Imagine the quarries of Indiana
seen from the air,
a knotted string on Lake Michigan's shore:
five synchronous hearts of an earthworm.)

His quarry teaches him to move:
dive without a splash, no scar to the surface,
stroke without air on his hands, to parcel
breath, atom by atom, into his limbs.
He learns an easy seriousness,

thinks of himself as water
(that resolved, that delicate)
when he begins to unionize the cutters
'behind his father's back,' a phrase
his father later uses
explaining bodily betrayal
by his blue-blood son. 'Unions gut
the free market.'

He leaves home for Silver Lake
in the White Mountains;
hopes to meet ee cummings
who has answered one of his letters

(Your interpretation of my 'blue-eyed boy'
is well put. Follow your instincts
about poetry, its words speak below the brain.
Helen kept that letter folded in her dictionary
under the letter P.)

cummings is dead, and Will
moves into the mountains to live
as he believes, a self-indulgent monk

slipping from lover to
lover, like a taste passed tongue
to tongue. Every woman he meets is too easy to love.

He chooses tasks that multiply rewards:
making bread, planting a garden, splitting logs.

Will, lazy as noon-time quarry water,
driven as a rain-swollen river.

Cathedral rises from the Seine,
a spiny fish.

Manon on the riverbank, selling her photographs —
in her shutter's instant
stone martyrs bleed dust, gargoyle spouts
like vultures over empty sidewalks —
a city in ruins.
They speak of beauty found in horror,
a pain Will wants to eat. He looks

because he will never see
through those eyes,
No tourist will buy these photographs.

Aren't you a tourist?

Together they walk Paris
exploring the marrow,
grey honeycomb, later
each other. Manon crawling as far into Will
as she can: a boat, his arms oars
stroking her out of the dark river.

When they are married Will sews
her wedding dress from a bolt
of yellow silk. To Manon the thread so bright
it might be the pollen
of a million bees
or juice from a grove of mangoes,
yellow as the sunflowers that turn their
faces, studded like sundials,
their stalks in fields,

in strict rows all over France.
(*Nazi flowers*, Helen said.)
A dress that has a cave taste.

A civil ceremony.
Afterwards they eat in an Italian restaurant,
pasta arrabiata, thick bread,
red wine. Manon bends across
the red-checked tablecloth
to Will, his cayenne lips.
The flame from the candle brightens
her face.

Chicago

Will wants them — Will, whose father
has disowned him for marrying a Jew.
Will, who never takes a job, who stays home
while Manon teaches high school.

Who wants children when life is a gift of loss?
They are more hope than Manon feels,
as promising as Chicago, glass
city built on flame-charred carapace.
Chicago, a trick with mirrors.

She vows she will speak to them
only of the cave, not of her war childhood,
a splinted bone.

Her children will never go to Europe, will live
in a landscape where glass obscures the ghosts.

Manon's photographs cover the walls.
All black and white
except the photos she has taken of the caves —
their colours sifted into her mind
like dust into eyes. Those pigments,
earth's memory of fire.

In the family photographs Manon looks
serious. Will, a clown.
In one Will holds France up
over his head.

Her fingers spread like blossoms
or sparks. Her mouth open as a balloon.
She floats over him
and he struggles to keep her on earth.
As if she were without mass,
pure air, or lighter,
noble gas.

France is born cold.
Blue fingers,
blue toes, her blood
won't circulate. When Helen is born
Will says, *We had Helen to keep France warm.*

Helen wants an audience, eager faces
over her crib. She cries
when they leave.
They move her into France's bed.
France, warmed. Helen, watched.

They will always sleep, France's body
on its left side, curved around Helen.
But Helen grows so fast, Manon worries
she will grow crooked, her body hardening
next to France, like candy
in a mold, her spine kinked, twisted
beside France's hips, stomach, chest,
a tendril round a stem.

France's body holding
Helen to the sun, this way
they blossom.

In university they play a game.
Each tries to choose one word
to make the other think
a memory they share.

Blue, Helen says. And France, *the eggs
in the nest outside our window.*
Yes. Yes.
Both of them back at that window,
back at the moment they find the nest
with two eggs.
Better than an Easter hunt,
blue as an ice cube, Helen says,
that's not blue, says France.
It's the truest blue.
No, the sky is bluest blue!
Every morning they watch
for a sign the chicks are hatching,
(crack, beak, a wet protruding wing).

One day the eggs are gone,
not a single shell in the nest.

Blue.

White tutu, white tights, spangled
leotard, wand, and crown, France wants
to be a fairy, but has outgrown her costume.
Helen wears it instead, an insect crawling
inside another's phosphorescent skin.
France wears a black T-shirt, black pants pinned at the joints
with the cut-out shapes of white felt bones.
A skeleton with blond hair.

Hand in hand along the sidewalk
careful to skip the cracks. Helen's crown droops
off her head, but she waves her wand,
touching and naming things
as she passes: *mailbox, tree, brick wall, fence.*

Looking down at her bones, France says, *This is what
it's like to be dead.* They pass a vacant lot,
Spooky, Helen says.
France drops down
on a pile of leaves — each one a fallen chapter
in the story of trees — *bury me.*

Lunar light spills, quicksilver, into earth-dark air.
Helen dances around France, touching her
with the wand, *I can bring you back to life.*
Bends on her knees over France, buries
her face in France's neck, *Don't scare me again.*

Leaves stuck to her luminous bones, each one a soul
clinging to a lost body.

⬎

A hunger strike

Helen: Nothing is fair.
Manon: Nothing is fair, eat your dinner.
Will: She has to live by what she believes.
Manon: She won't live if she doesn't eat.

Almost Helen's eighth birthday, and
someone tells her African children
are dying. Someone shows her
their faces, big faces,
eyes swollen, necks too thin to hold
their heads. She wears a bloated
pillow under her T-shirt — their stomachs are puffed,
she cannot explain why hungry stomachs get bigger,
don't vanish, like necks, arms, legs.

Helen is grandstanding, she hasn't
learned the world doesn't care
what she thinks.

For two days she stares at a clean
dinner plate. France takes seconds,
Helen has left me for something brighter.

⬎

Why do you have to fly at night?
Helen asks, tucked into bed.
How can the airplane see?
Her sister laughing, *airplanes don't need to see.*
And their father, *France, don't laugh.*
France remembers his words, the strain on him
of scolding her. And Helen, his voice,
the weight of him on the bed, how she rolls
towards the edge where he sits.

Their parents will fly across an ocean
to Europe. Helen wiggles.
Who will take care of me?
Manon will photograph the caves again.

They will always smell
their mother: smoke. Her hair falling over them
in bed, smoky from the fireplace. They will
remember her as a smell,
animal to them, having absorbed the fire
into her skin, into all that hair
falling over them.

After the crash, they never speak of her
to each other. They suffer separate
guilt that they remember
only her smell. That smoke hair.

Around them the plane's whirr, murmur
of those who cannot sleep. Manon reads —
a small cup of light poured
onto her book
and Will's head on her
shoulder, a shadow across the page —
sentences march into and out of his darkness.

Around the circle of light brightening
this embrace, a larger circle of darkness — the aisles,
the plane's humped seats, snug overhead
compartments — beyond that the metal
husk, chill night air, and then numb,
childless galaxy.

Will dreams, Manon's story, perhaps, rambling
the haunted planets
of his sleep. And the plane dreams too

it is bursting, peeling back
the night's skin,
raw wound.
For a moment a whole constellation
burns there, then their bodies
fall, flaming, these wanderers reeling over themselves.
Gemini.

Jews can't go to heaven
Marcia announces. Helen kicks leaves piled
along gutters. *Jesus invented it,
you have to believe in him to get in.*

Suddenly this news:
their parents are separated. One
in heaven, one in the place that burns.

Unbearable to imagine their parents halved —
I don't believe it, Helen says.
Jesus doesn't care if you believe it,
Marcia's book bag swinging
back and forth, *it's the truth,* sun sliding
down the sky.

Foster home
Evanston, Illinois

So many hours France
stands between two walls of

floor to ceiling mirrors,
an endless corridor, she is
endless chorus girl for once

keeping time. Behind the mirrors
lurk closets she can
slip inside, dreaming, she stares at

blankness through an opening.
The white hallway, solitude.
Always, her dumb face intrudes.

Here parents exploded, but numb-skull
mirrors don't show that,
make her exist.

She has to fool the mirrors, cover her body
in mirrors, so it is all outside, pure glitter,
fierce shine. She stands

the mirrored girl in the mirrored hall,
staring at nobody, nobody, nobody

A cave in the suburbs

Helen finds a crack in a cliff that gushes
air, just enough for a small
body to squeeze through. Besides, the other games
are tired, there is no need for school,
their parents are dead.
Everyone is afraid to give them rules. The foster
parents' one rule: sleep alone.
A rule that has to be
broken.

(No one could bear to lie down in darkness.
The pictures that appear
on your eyelids, and all those stars
billions of miles apart
spinning in breathless space.)

The cave is the answer
to emptiness, a way to join two halves.
This time Helen brings oil and France.
Take off your clothes.
        Helen, we shouldn't, we'll get in trouble.
Come on, no one will know.
They smear themselves with Wesson oil
Helen then France,
part by part,
one leg and arm, stomach, chest,
nipples pushing like hazelnuts in cake,
finally her head scrapes its ear against rock
Helen inside pulling France's
leg like a dog. Her hand
strains to claw away dirt
so her skull can pass,
and finally she pulls herself in.

They drag in a flashlight,
a tuna sandwich, the book
of photographs given to them
by their mother, pictures of cave walls.
A note she wrote stuck in the page
with a drawing of two reindeer:
one kneeling, the other bending
to lick its forelock.
Are you taking care of each other?

So much is made to be broken.

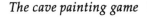

The cave painting game

They flex their bodies
into shapes that cast silhouettes
like animals. Magic, crawl inside,
make the animals move. Like letters
in calligraphy suddenly
elevating from the page, walking
on tiny mosquito legs —
reindeer, bear, fish, horse, mammoth —
they bring into the cave
to strut, grin, scream
(fingers make long teeth).

Even France makes angry
creatures if Helen is there.

One photograph: a ring
of bison etched into a deep hollow
in the cave. The foot of one is a part
of the neck of another, two joined
at the rump.

It's like Siamese, France says.
What's that? Helen asks.

Babies born at the same time who share
parts of their bodies.
Sometimes their brains.

When I have a baby, Helen says, *I want one.*

⌒

France steers, her hands under Helen
who is on the handlebars.
From a distance they look like
a two-headed monster.
I can't feel my fingers, France says
and Helen, *my butt hurts.*
Hold on, France upright on her pedals,
breathless, sucking air into sharpened lungs, *we're almost*
there. They ease over,
coast down, France dragging
her tennis shoes to slow them.

There it is, see the plane! Prepare for takeoff.
Tower, do we have clearance? Final checks, okay!
Helen hops down, watches France
who flicks switches on the invisible control
panel before her.

The Cessna, accelerating.
Duck — Helen, for once, frightened.
France stands up straight, salutes the pilot,
gawks at the plane's smug belly.

Holy, holy,
he waved at me!

LAB NOTES
VANCOUVER AQUARIUM

Winter 1992

I work from photographs of skeletons.
Blue whale, Sei whale.

From dissection notes on a minke fetus.
Nothing done before refers to this work.

Bones compose a vanished body. Speak a language
thin as air.

⌒

This one found rotten, beached with plastic bottles, suntan
oil, hypodermic needles, rubble of this century.

I tear ripe meat, boil the bones in sodium carbonate, spray
bleach. Beside my workroom, the orcas in a whale jail, a
cube of processed sea — they circle, again, again. I hear the
tape played outside, the singing of living whales. Soon my
dead whale will hang, screech and laughter of their gossip
whirling between its bones.

I imagine what living tissue held them. And I hear Helen's
voice, her loon-laugh, keen scratching of the migrating dead,
like wind on a sail or airplane wing.

Helen is with the dead. With my father, gone before I knew
him. I grew up staring at his photograph: *Private Peter H—,
Canadian Armed Forces.* He had a secret only I might
understand. Since I had his name. Hence, *private.*

But if I invented a thousand languages I could never speak
to the man in the photograph. My childhood spent groping
for words, the bones that made them, letters like snakes and
ladders, a route to him.

And my adulthood?
Searching for a tunnel to Helen.

Note: to be reread when I am too sentimental.

You cannot outrun the dead. They are in the elements —
even at my birth, Lake Ontario was dying. From the
Thousand Islands to the bilge harbours of Hamilton where I
grew up, it unspooled itself. Restless as a virus. Terminal.
Sludge waters from treatment plants fed bacterial blooms.
No oxygen. Nuclear reactors, hydroelectric plants pimpling
the long stretch of concrete from Bowmanville through
Scarborough, Toronto, Hamilton, to Niagara-on-the-Lake.
The river slipping away to sea, carrying secret waste.

3 a.m.

I am a well-oiled machine, she said,
Molotov cocktail, bomb
when there's nothing else: bottle, gasoline, rag.

Thick black clouds over Iraq. Kuwait.
Chicago too.

Don't think of her face. Wait. Don't breathe.

Morning

Shouldn't every word have its place, shouldn't
language flow between us to be
understood? A body built
when we speak.

Articulation. Each word snapped
into its joint. Verbs like tendons,
levering, moving nouns ridged
with calcium. Prepositions, knuckles.
Articles, nails. Words fixed
to the things they are.

And when there's misunderstanding, when
I have that bone to pick with you,
shouldn't words convey exactly
meaning?

Later

Her private words for everything.

Night flight, making love.
Oroboros, 69.

There were *Fascists*, anyone who wasn't
left-wing. *The Saint*, Chomsky.
Twin, France, though they were not.
She said they were Siamese twins, I
didn't know how to see.
My eyesight always an issue between us.

Once I described one to her, she called
herself *The Jew Fish*. How could I want
to be a scientist. All the horror
done in the name of science.
They weren't scientists, I said.

Condom, *raincoat*. Her guitar, *Bird*.
Class, *sleep therapy*.
Menstruation, *The Last Supper*.

She had a word for when I held her in my arms.
Standing at the sink, my wrists
under hot water,
                    I can't remember.

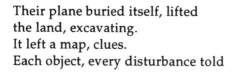

How did I come to this whale?

Long ago I gave up looking for my father. I wandered
Hamilton's docks, learned ropes and charts. They gave
answers — maps told depths, the name of a lighthouse,
its flash and moan. Pull a halyard, see it raise the sail. A
sheet attaches to the clew. Mysteries explained: ships sail
into wind, the Bernoulli Effect. The angle between a light
on shore and the mast will change if the anchor drags.

If I tucked myself away, studied, answers would be given.

My sister lived in Boston with a husband, two kids. *Get away
from Hamilton, Ontario, Nowhere-land. Adjust yourself. Forget
alley ways. Learn to speak differently. Watch TV*, she said, *learn
to set a table, throw a dinner party.*

In Chicago I found a spark. And Helen. Her green world.
Her brightness.

Their plane buried itself, lifted
the land, excavating.
It left a map, clues.
Each object, every disturbance told

something. Scientists were called in.
As time spiralled
away, they fought to fold
it back. Insisting chaos has its
pattern.

I am the scientist gaping at the crash site
making notes.
As if corpses made sense.
As if the second law of thermodynamics
could be broken.

≈⟩

A Valentine's poem

For months of nights, what I did
was not die, sleepless on the futon,
beer, television's blurred eye
nursing my panic.

Drifting to work in the morning,
glad distraction, at last tired, even
forgetting what clutched me
in the half-light of waking sleep.

(The clock with its always
ticking.) My mother visited from out of town,
didn't ask what was wrong,
my face betrayed me.

She took me to the beach.
Seaweed slag littered the snow like dog shit
and rocks wore the puny wings
of seagull carcasses. The sea,

one more way of erasing. From inside the hot
restaurant we watched it scrape the sand
scrape the sand,
             at 4 a.m.

I write this, tasting the clams my mother ate,
the kind my father loved, the inside soft
like woman or worm as it entered her mouth, then
the ghost whisper of tires

warming the slick surface
of the road. We stopped at a gas station.
My mother eyed the attendant,
another woman who stayed up at night, worrying

about a child. (Mothers prepare
themselves for holocaust. Nightly
mine plotted routes to bomb shelters, food. Armed
us with topographical maps —

my sister and I would stumble towards her
from opposite ends of the continent.)
But there she was in the midst of dark night,
my mother, who could sing through anything, who could

keep me alive. All the way home,
my mother had her hands
on the wheel, fighting off death,
as I slept, dreamless.

Do I have Will wrong? What did either of them tell me
about him? Quarries, cummings, Will's lazy beauty.
And Manon? They had to guess, she told so little.

While Manon's mother pushed her
from her body into the painted cave,
scientists were busy across the valley. In a game
to ghost-scare themselves
four boys and a dog stumbled into Lascaux.
Animals emerged as if dreamt by the stone

(Manon, dust in a dust cave — a half-life)

underground river of ghostly herds.

If a story doesn't rub off on you, then it is a lie.
If it does not marrow in,
oily, greased, do not trust it. If the ink
does not sweat the page, if it does not moisten
fingertips, wrists, that naked
edge of palm, curled, pressed against
paragraph, if there is no dark mark,
whale-shaped, then truth has fled.

FIRST-YEAR UNIVERSITY

Helen wears white robes, powders her face
till her dark eyes scour, predatory. Her movements
on stage are stiff — all elbows.

Relax, the director instructs, *try to feel the part*.

She kneels, pretends to scrape the ground for dirt;
she must cover her brother's grave.
Her brother, lover.
She auditions for grief — scratches
at the floor, pleads,
What life is there for me without him?
The director breaks in, *There's no line there*.

*But that's what Antigone would say,
she has to say something*.

Say it with your body, the director says,
then we'll be eating out of your hands.

Helen bends again, furiously scraping,
the folds of her robe rippling over
her back, she bends her head forward,
as a woman washing her hair will bend her neck,
her fingers clutching, clutching
invisible grains, sifting them, dusting
over the imagined grave.

How we meet

Everyone pours beer from the same pitcher.
Helen pours for me, I look sad.
I always look sad, it's the way my face falls.

Already she favours me
I need rescuing.
*The birds don't migrate
from the cities any more,* I say, gazing through
steamed windows as a pair of Canada geese across the street
shuffle through plastic bags, wound-red leaves.
The city's too warm.

They don't mate for life, either, she says. *Too much
lead in the lake water. Even swans
are promiscuous.*

We walk home under an empty sky.
Nothing guides us but desire.

Together in her single bed, she is above
me, arms outstretched beyond our heads,
fingers spread, comets.

Hard bones beneath her skin press
   my hip, collarbones, ribs,
against her, I might be shipwrecked —

I do not resist the waves or rock, the treasures
they carry. Helen, a worn shard of green glass.

*How do the birds find their way
when they migrate?*

Stars, I say. *No matter how the
night sky rotates, birds will orient
to the North Star. They read the stars
like a map. Carry the knowledge in genes.*

I don't tell her: the heart of every cell is
etched with the pattern of stars — a chart
for night flight.

She wants me to take my glasses off, but I
won't. I have to see her to make love.

She believes in the blind
lover, wants someone who knows her
by smell, by her curious geography:
that long neck,
her collarbones, glacial,
left at her shoulders by receding
ice. A sensory lover. All intuition.

I know she needs an explorer willing to
enter whatever wildness
she presents, to match it
with curiosity's sharp blade.

Because I am that explorer, because I
have crossed bridges and borders
to come to her country, I convince her
to trust the lover who sees.

She talks so much, to know what she says
I have to read her frantic gestures.
Her semaphore.

You're like my mother with her camera, she says,
*a piece of glass, a lens between you
and the world. Not to see more clearly,
but to obscure. To keep your private
world. A room with a closed door.*

She knows that much about me.

Helen says her parents were killed by terrorists. Says it
      matter-of-fact. Terror,
word like a dog begging on hind legs, t-error, a cross and
      then error. Why the false courage,
unflinching? Why finish her sentence, *Terrorists acting in
      retaliation against terror by the United States?*
My parents were complicit, she says, *didn't do enough to stop the
      government from what it did.* Why blame the victims?
She doesn't want her own parents dead.
      To make sense, so the pieces fit? Or,
worse, because she is jealous, wakes one morning in love
      with grand death, finding her own skull
delicious? Her sister smothers every fire, forgives, forgives,
      forgives, why not blame someone or take blame?
It is one way to behave.

      For an instant, beside her, I might be alive.

She loves me in snow, the thick
falling of it, ashes or hands
full of hair, it falls
as a swimmer pushing air
into water from her fingers.
In snow, our first winter at college,
we have slept together
on and off for months.
But tonight I smell of steel mills, great
lakes, and gasoline, someone she can measure
her life against. She thinks I am as strong
and righteous as her father — loves me in snow
because in spite of it she can smell

what she thinks I am, can bury herself, alive,
as the snow is alive, aching down,
milled onto us.

To come after so many months
to the realization of love. Something
to taste, put your teeth on.
My shoulders, ball and socket, the purr
of gears, love, a machine
(not something soft to be startled from)
love, screaming down highways or
jetting into firmament. Love moves,
slips away, is transmission.

She leans into me in the snow, pressing me
against the car parked outside the bar. Reaches
her hands up against my bare skin, blood
pulse, the heart engine.

How each argument
makes Helen more
beautiful

That scientist saw her theory of menstruation in a dream, Helen
says, *black triangles floating down a river of blood, she knew the
blood was for cleansing what the penis carries into a woman.*
    *That isn't how science works, you choose one story, about
one scientist to prove science a fantasy. Your method is flawed.*
I want to provoke her anger, those fluttering hands, sharp
elbows are passion. They might signal a passion for me.
    No, she says, *there was that German man, he dreamed of
Oroboros, a snake biting its own tail, he woke knowing benzene's
structure is a ring.*

Did he invent 69?

Dancing to Lou Reed and cooking dinner, we weave through the kitchen. Making pasta, Helen doesn't eat meat (nothing with a face). We drink too much wine. *Wine takes practice*, I say. *Commitment*, says Helen.

I measure precisely, *You use too many spices.* I tell Helen about bread, *it's all biochemistry. The yeast cells consume sugar, producing carbon dioxide, sometimes ethanol. We let the yeast eat, then we eat them. Life is just electricity —*

She knows I'm baiting her, *My father told me, if you eat a watermelon seed with a piece of bread and drink a cup of water, a vine will rise out of your throat. You have to believe, Peter.* She puts her hands over my eyes, *yours would never grow without me.*

⁓

France in the sky

France loves two things: her sister
and the sky, she drops

out of college, spends nights as a cocktail
waitress, days at the airstrip —
the lake's concrete skirt. A man
teaches her to 'fly by wire.'

Sometimes she has to
fuck him, but not too often,
(she doesn't look at his face)
and he offers:
                    howling
wind streaming past wings, pleasure
of lift over things, the fuselage settling
buoyant. She digs the upward tug
to sun's gold burn,

the sky pushes her into herself
like a great mirror — sends her back
inside again, again

She swallows, feels the quiver in her
throat, whole body quaking. Pockets
of pressure lift or drop
she has to concentrate.

He leans across the controls,
presses teeth, lips into her neck,
barks, *fly me, precious.*

⁀⁀

Fairytale

There are no parents, only twins alone in a forest filled with
wolves. There may be a trail, but it will be made of crumbs.
There may be a house, but it will hide a cage of bones.

Helen's last summer (the months before the invasion) is
the last summer of childhood. It is a long field, filled with
tall grass — they walk through it together. Those flowers, life
in all its sweet and strange configurations. Two sisters without
parents, they find each other miraculous; so fragile, delicately
scented, they are learning to turn their faces into wind.

They lie in the mornings on the bed in the apartment on
56th Street, cups of coffee propped on their stomachs. Helen
is taking classes that summer, and France is finally learning
to skydive. It is hot by 9 a.m., so they jam open the door to
the fire escape, there are alley cats out there that sniff the
catnip Helen grows for them, a small fan blows air through
the door and steam from the coffee into their noses.

Sometimes Helen talks about me. She thinks she loves me,
and so one day she asks, *Do you think they loved each other?*
France knows Helen means their parents, and so she has
broken the rule between them and spoken of the dead.

I don't know, France says. She remembers her parents in pieces: father's face, mother's scent. She doesn't think she understands anything but sister-love.

I know they did. I see them like that, falling through the air holding each other's hand.

꩜

Quick as a firefly, impossible
to trap. Helen burns
a trail behind her. She has no patience
for long words, they take too long to say,
her words reduced to syllables.

A breakfast of pancakes, blueberries, and yogurt
becomes *cakes, bloobs, and yogs.*
In the same way she rarely says my whole name.
It is *P.* Sometimes *Sweet P,*
or *I gotta take a pee, P.* She loves the variations.
When you take my hand in marriage, she says, pouring batter
onto the pan, *you'll have to take my name too, P Green.*

I listen for silences between her words
but there are none. She titrates language
to its basic elements. Scolds me because I
won't play. I say, *What words can you make with H?*
You are hydrogen, the first element,
one electron, one proton. Monogamous
attraction — the only fate I believe in.

Pleased, she says, *Set the periodic*
table for be-fast.

꩜

She goes down deep
into emptiness, crawling into a diamond
cave,
            a hole entirely of light.

            In the brief
moment before parachute,
                                    as she rushes,
accelerating, anticipating the brakes
                        of friction, breathing, spirituous, into

terminal velocity
                        that moment,

still as a lake, as the chute unfurls,
                                    an anchor line,
            silent,
                        time unscrolls too,
arranges its brushes, paints,
                        time hangs
                                    a long mirror.
            France is alone.

If a twin is a mirror, the sky is too.

In that second: something adoring
that gazes back at you
with your own grin, that gives you to you.

That touches.

When it catches, you can think
of other things. Other people even.

The heat is a cat that smothers you
in her fur, heat crawls, thick cream
over the city. We sit on the stoop
eating watermelon, spitting seeds
into dark. Voices carry at night:
laughter, lovemaking, rage, children playing
hide 'n' seek between buildings, under cars,
in garbage mounds.
Sirens knife the air.

We walk hand in hand along the lake.
Past abandoned high-rises,
boarded up windows, against headlights
of Lakeshore Drive.
Sometimes cars turn into parking lots
teenagers looking for a place
to drink. Setting radios on car hoods
they dance, their cigarettes fireflies in dark.

Past the museum, we see the park that lies
between lake and city, its virgin,
its debutante. Where the park is
the old city was, Old Chicago, burned
to the ground when a cow tipped over a lamp.

The city sparks behind us, tiara,
its rotten tunnels invisible in the dark.

At the planetarium, we pull off our clothes,
moulting dragonflies we leave
a lost skin behind,
glide out from the stone shore, and swim.
The heat in our skulls pushes
down arms and legs
into the icy water.
When we can at last see the lights

of stars, we dive below the surface
into the lake's dark hole.

Peter, a star-ladle spoons out the lake.

Each star is a sustained nuclear explosion.

Floating on our backs, we touch soles
paddle in circles,
pretend giant fish eat our legs.
I clutch Helen's waist:
Help, I'm in love and I can't swim.

LAB NOTES
VANCOUVER AQUARIUM

Summer 1992

She cut the drawing from one of my books.
I was furious, *who gave you the right?*
> *Books need to have lives,* she said.

*I suppose you think you're
the whale?* I was angry with her.

*I'm the one at the oars — I'm going to carry
it in my pocket, give
it to someone who needs it.*

You are the ice —

Sometimes there is no bone.
The maggots or the chemicals
have eaten it away.
Only a gap remains.
I build bones
from whatever makes sense: fibre-
glass, foam, epoxy for car repairs.
I sculpt what I imagine
or the mirror-twin of one I have.
I paint the bone bone-coloured.

*Marginalia found in Helen's
copy of H. D.*

Last night P gave me a ruby-red
dress. Tight as skin.
Lifting me in his arms, Cinnamon!
Dynamite! Licorice stick!
Fire Engine!
Spinning round.
He accepts my delights
and rages. Understands fission
the intricate circulation
of warm-blooded fish — I would risk
my heart to him

                              though he has
no politics — something he claims
Canadian — he wants me to love him more
than justice — imagine

France says I'm a fool
not to love him this instant. Says
she isn't jealous, exactly.
I can live with this!

I find the book flying across the room
just then I know the limit —
what the skull will endure.

∽

Neck thrown
back to laugh. One coral button I cut
from her dress
(I have spent hours carrying it in my mouth).
A word she gave me from her private language
(a word like *bee-lush* that meant the colour
of her mother's wedding dress, or *tendrilly,*
how she slept beside me).

I was looking for her, and there she was.
Below me, swimming in my blue
cereal bowl.
I can eat every atom of her
and she will live. I will build my bones
from her bread.

I move my spoon, a rake in cold ashes
lift sweet grains —
sunlight through the basement window
in a square on the linoleum table, a breeze
that lifts the curtains.

How easy grief would be
if you made each meal from the dead.

∽

I think suddenly about my father. I must telephone him, tell him about Helen, make appropriate introductions. Then, just as suddenly I know that he would have my voice. I would hear myself speaking through the long crackling wire from the other, burning side.

All my life, in every moment, he has been both present and absent. Intangible as the wind that pushes the sail, he haunts me, in some feature of my own face or hands, tilt of my hips, even my penis — as if he speaks in my body as desire.

Wind erodes the soft rock revealing the hardest ores — he lives inside me. His genes, their chemical semaphore — each amino acid a flag — the only language he and I will ever share.

In me, his lost body floats up, a private moon.

My mother will say, *you look so much like your father.* Then I want to chisel his features from my face, flesh from my flesh, to have him appear in me as he is, a hole the size of a man.

Does Helen speak to him now — mistake him for me?

Stanley Park
June

Get up to walk the dog, sunny day
but the sky somehow blank
with a nail-clipping of moon
out of place. Green in every leaf,
sticky, unfolding, the swarm of bud
and bee. Colour mocks me.

Get up from the page, though
pictures insist themselves
even in this landscape.
(All morning news reports of the trial.
A schoolgirl slain. They keep saying *schoolgirl*.)
All those pictures beamed into summer green.

We can't banish what we carry
disembodied in our heads.
Helen, that girl float to the surface, bob up,
uncurl like chestnut leaves.

A man on the path stops me. How long has it been
since I spoke to someone? Why choose me?
In long white pants, long white sleeves,
collar buttoned up though the day is hot.
He speaks with troubled breathing,
　　　I used to keep horses.
My dog a shepherd.
He was curious, went into the stall when a foal was born
the birth still wet in the hay, and his paws
soaked with blood.
Dogs are curious, foals are curious, they touched
each other nose to nose.

After that, when the foal went into the pasture
that dog would position himself between the foal
and the geldings. If the geldings went near
he would stand on hind legs, raise up a storm.
I never trained that dog.

Go back to the beast,
　　　　　　enter it.

Galileo prayed the stars were
a handwriting. If he could
solve the orbits, he might know
God's mind. As a boy, I dreamt of uncoding
stars, satellites. Dot and dash.

You can die without
having prepared an idea of death.

I hold the flat atlas bone
in hand. Hole in the centre
for the spinal cord, a cable
between the body's desires, the head's intent.
A living fuse.

I woke this morning startled. No
dreams of Helen. My sleep
forgets her.

In the spinal cord there survive the circuits
for a muscle speech.
Even if the brain dies the cord
remembers familiar gestures — hands
clasped in prayer, military salute,
the hand to the heart —
a longing without intellect, like a tide,
tug towards God, country, lover,
the idea each cell has for another.

As if the spinal cord holds the fossil
record: what's touched us, what love
has moved in the compartments of our blood.

Did I say Helen held me, did I
make it clear, say that she reached across the table
placed my fingers between hers, palms touching,
across table, beside the cup of cigarette
butts, empty glasses, dried remains
of beer, she grabbed my hand, the candle
brightening her face, said,
I know how that is,
she held me with those hands,
it was the night I met her,
did I say she tried to love me?

I know what the stars say: there is nothing
either good or bad — only entropy.

At lunch, desiring light, I leave the basement.
Before I can escape I must pass the whale tank.
Their circling endless as grief.

The male's limp dorsal fin droops down his back —
the female has dropped a still birth into the tank.
They have left her dead infant floating
she prods it over and over, her cries
bounce off concrete,
wave upon wave of her own wails crash
crazy back into her ears,
she is dis-located by her echo.

A crowd peers in through the huge windows
on the side of the tank, their faces
are flowers pressed against glass, children held
up like offerings.

How grotesque love's prisons.

In the middle of repairing the split
nasal bone — fragile work, much
concentration — I remember,
she called it *caveful* when I held her in my arms,
when I could feel her ribs, lungs clenched.
Caveful, like careful, she said, *only with a wider embrace.*
She was beloved there, watched over.

Though it was Will's strength she craved,
she was like Manon,
and I am too, always dreaming of something
wondrous overhead:
dozens of cloth sails billowing,
collecting into their folds.

A lullaby world — green hull, anchor.

My whale will live in air, float,
gargoyle, above human heads. It will
have no secrets, nothing to hide.
Parents will bring children
to learn something. There will be
measurements, dates, location, its name,
Balaenoptera acutorostrata,

there will be a card in the card catalogue,
entry in the thick ledger book locked
in the aquarium's catacombs (a book
with the names of the dead).
There will be facts to explain everything.
No one will be listening.

One child will leave her parents behind,
roam from the maps to a circle
of tile under the whale. She will raise her face
to a space between ribs:
room to hide in. She has never
loved anything so big, never felt she could be eaten
and live. What a suite
the whale is
and the girl, its anchoress.
She lies back on its ribs,
prepares tea in cups of ivory,
she sleeps, dreams a long
bone bed, she wakes,
is never scared of darkness again.

AFTER THE INVASION 1990

France dreams of falling
from the sky, over and over,
that second in a slight
tumult of air
she loses faith, can't believe in the chute,
its billowing palm, arresting her free
fall. She dreams it again, again
that second of doubt.
                Then her back
finds its claws, spins a web into sky,
she slows, plumping.
                      Lift then drag.

She can see the map of land below her
like all reports on the TV screen.
Until then she didn't know she knew
the names of those countries: *Jordan,*
Saudi Arabia, Iraq, Kuwait
she sees herself falling into the letters on the map
into the names of those places.
She has come to rescue the citizens, once she reaches
the ground, she will know how to behave.

She is down, people swarm,
touching her hair, her skin. Children
circle her, fingering the chute's bright silk.
She has no way back.
No way home. And she cannot help —
she is one of them.

Leaves swirl in the empty fountain
Students wander the quadrangle, one

deep inside the last pages of a book
steps
into the fountain
out again
without looking up.

Helen watches squirrels, their leaps and scurries
through grass, up trunks, along branches,
tracing the tree's body,
tired napkins and candy wrappers
in their teeth. Around her, white stone
buildings, ornate, crenellations crowded with gargoyles,
stone curls, buttresses. *These buildings should sag,*
something has to happen, someone has to witness it.

Crimson leaves are a warning.
Even the chilled flowers
in their orderly beds
threaten her with bloom.

The paper says:
. . . *Military action authorized*
against Iraq unless it ends
its occupation of Kuwait by January 15.

Swaying back and forth, trembling,
she crawls into herself —
I begin to lose her.

Jangle near my temple, black nerve,
stupid root, I snap on
the light, press the phone
to my ear, Helen's voice,
watery, charged
particles breaking into discord.

My friend Marcia just called me,
guess what she said?

My eyes follow the blinking
blue clock, power must have gone out.
Marcia joined the CIA, Langley,
that's what they call it.
She writes reports for human aid.
In the blue light I watch my fingers push
through the spiralling hole
of the telephone cord, *So? Helen,*
it's the middle of the night.

She can't read. They won't let
her read anything unless it's approved.

Come over, Helen, I need to see your face.
I'm sick of politics —

Then someone else owns you
it's us against them, fire with fire —

Last Party

Helen, plays Bird, singing
so bitter and so sweet, arguing
Canadians are the best lyricists — it's in their genes.
You should know that, turning to me.
She will claim preposterous
things — is she kidding?

Head thrown back, strange
wailing laugh.

She convinces France to dance.
When they do, love
alights in the room, swirls
in Helen's skirt, France's ankles.

I watch the creature
they make together, desiring
the body formed
in their shadow against the wall.

≋

Television from the desert

Film crews move in.
Bodies assemble
in her living room. Uniforms. Sand.
She can't adjust the fine tuning. Lines
on the glass, dust motes.
She pleads on knees to voices behind
the screen, *someone throw something, a switch*
she wants to confess to the screen, have the thing
absolved, wants absolution herself, wave
after wave of panic, static
electricity, the long deaf ear
of the television tube, nothing
travels back that way,

what if Chicago is next,
what if they have the bomb?

No, isn't it easy —
they are only a dream,
no one will really die, bombs
are *smart* and *surgical*,
their trace, the Milky Way, and people expire
eventually, and she can't sleep, because

the smell in her living room is
this century,
tires buried underground
catch fire, smouldering.

⁓

They play their game. *Centipede*, France says.

The mirrors in the hallway,
says Helen. *Yes*, says France.
Yes.

After they were adopted out,
they would stand between
the mirrors at the foster home

France behind Helen or
Helen behind France

making a long creature
with infinite, wiggling arms.

Where did the body stop?

Yellow, says Helen.
Her wedding dress?

No, the yellow ribbons.

⁓

Fill the streets, fill the streets,
someone is listening,

they call out to each other, as they walk,
Helen holding my hand and the hand
of an accountant.

We hold each others' hands and sleeves,
walk the streets from the Grant Park
fountain to Daley Plaza, chanting
prayers and curses, saying, *Stop the War.*

My father would be proud, Helen says,
France should have come.

I was too weak to stay away.

She thinks someone is listening,
thinks they can raise the price of war too high,
she marches to say, *Peace*
she means this

breathing the air of others
to fill her body, breathing, and
holding on.

LAB NOTES
VANCOUVER AQUARIUM

August 1992

In today's paper, photographs
at the university in Chicago
where the first nuclear chain reaction
was conducted underneath
bleachers beside the gridiron.
They decorated Moore's mushroom-cloud
monument with thousands of paper cranes.
Hiroshima's anniversary.
Origami cranes, small as atoms, strung
into strands, draped like chains
over the metal cloud.

(A girl dying of cancer folded
a thousand paper cranes,
a charm to cure herself.)

Some chemistry professors developed soft
skulls, hair grew grey as ashes
while they worked. Their dream
of chains, a snake
nursing on the tip of its tail,
unstable nuclei, paring
themselves down, splitting off neutrons.

Fission. Critical mass. They dreamt
the halo around stars,
all that is not iron,
what chaos there was that could be coupled,
satisfied, energy built from nuclei
driven by light speed.

Science boiled up new ways to die:
bodies transformed into photographic light.

(I am no scientist. Not one of that rank. I am Jew Fish.)

Today, the pilot of the Enola Gay
has flown back for Hiroshima's
Ash Anniversary
for his moment in
history, to meet the survivors,
touching down
in that shadow city.

～

A decision about science

We are always falling
(and things falling through us — others,
those beloved) with fingers open
(and mouths) trying to catch air
(which science has told us is full,
not empty) which feels full
when we reach for it

and becomes empty.
How *whole* has *hole* inside

because language mocks.

So sisters often fall in love,
seeing themselves in each other, knowing
'the love that might make me one.'

Name the groping:

I yell to the future
it returns as past.

～

A dream of hands.
A dream of hands cut off, sticking
in concrete fished from
lake silt, blue
hands wedged in snowbanks, hands
with five fingers, hands, only palms,
a dream of hands
as signposts planted in ground, a hand
with a helmet hung lonely from it,
hands that are the branches of trees,
storm torn. A dream of hands
as furniture, hands of wheat,
hands given in marriage,
handles on luggage, finger bowls,
a dream in which the hand asks,
do you want your fortune told?
Hands, built by industry.

Analysis: to write of her is to raid her grave.
Dismember. In English 'remember' means
to put the body together again.

Precisely through the centre, marrow
spiralling off the steel bit I press into vertebrae, shoulders
hunched, arms flexed, I sprout wings
fashioning postures of death,
each bone to be strung on a long metal rod bolted to
the skull, each vertebra strung like a bead
in a child's game. The rod hangs, expectant,
swaying on ropes from a ceiling beam,
hangs lonely, waiting for me to put the body

in order, to make it whole
from memory, if I
deny this end, if I make the order
different, connections where there were
no connections, if I tell lies,
biological impossibilities, a new rough
beast will be given a name.

In Spanish, *recordar*, to pass back through the heart.

JANUARY 1991

Starlings live in Helen's walls,
they crawl into pockets where stones
have gone missing,
feeling heat, feeling need,
birds feather their nests —

Her heat leaks, luxurious, gold
filtering into snowfall.
Like a lover, it begs them to stay.
Through the walls, they stutter praises
back and forth, twittering.

Nests lined with feathers
like the coats of royalty, feathers loosed
from the breast and wings. Feathers braided
with twigs.

Helen nestles in my arms, whispers,
All night the birds dream
beside ourselves, dreaming all night of birds.

They infect her dreams,
stockpiling weapons. Borders
crossed at night. Soldiers
in aircraft carriers, trucks, barracks, planes.
A dream informed
by military intelligence — possible deaths
are numbered and named.
Plotted by scientists.
Years before, staged by the four-star General
in a simulation. The Tomahawk cruise
missile travels
from the New England Patriots' stadium
to a stadium in New York and flies
through the goal posts,

a Patriot missile *the first hero*
of this war defeats a Soviet built SCUD,
Abrahms tanks shoot through Iraqi
armaments and are *tested for future conflicts*
by punishing Arabian sand,
Apache helicopters at night, in bad weather
seeing
with infrared eyes, France leaping
down the sky, a dream
of arms, men
and women clutch
M-16s to fight AK-47s.
A camera flies
on a missile's nose into a building
defined in sites and crosshairs

the consumer asks:
how long is my satellite delay?

⮑

Decorations: T-shirt of an Iraqi bent over, his pants pulled
down, *Saddam-ize Hussein*, SCUD lollipops and jaw breakers,
Patriot missile T-shirts, posters, buttons, gas masks *(be a*
survivor), Hussein toilet paper, Persian Gulf interactive
video game. *Support Our Troops.* Cartoons of bearded men
running from Uncle SAM, M-16 water pistols, banners,
balloons, Arab voodoo dolls, yellow ribbons on American
lampposts, American trees — if I could walk back across the
border I would, but there's Helen — they consume the war
in jubilee.

⮑

France in love

France, beside him
in the van filled with diving equipment.
They are on top of a parachute.
She vows never to count on it to anchor
her in air. He has worked
the condom off, placed it beside her ear,
it cradles drops like pearls, fluid
smooth as silky chute. His beard scratches
her, he has fallen
asleep on her numb arm,
a puddle of drool near the corner of his mouth
seeping onto her nipple. Moving her eyes
to the rear windows, she watches
a passing sky fill with pellets of sleet, windows
begin to freeze in lace patterns.
She is chilly in the sheet of parachute.
She looks at him
vapour rising from his mouth
like sky writing.
He might, after all, be beautiful.

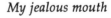

My jealous mouth

Bush is at peace with himself,
Bush is at peace.
The war is coming. It makes me sick.
Can't they see. Men and women burning
in slow fire, friendly fire. I hate the word
casualties.

Nothing is casual, I say.

And dead-line? Don't they listen
to their own mouths? I can't eat, Helen says,
I feel sick at my own hunger. It's unfeeling.

It's not your responsibility
a war has stolen her from me.

Peter, this is my war.

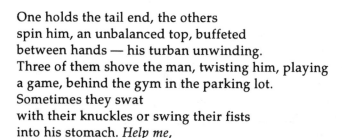

One holds the tail end, the others
spin him, an unbalanced top, buffeted
between hands — his turban unwinding.
Three of them shove the man, twisting him, playing
a game, behind the gym in the parking lot.
Sometimes they swat
with their knuckles or swing their fists
into his stomach. *Help me*,
he gasps. *He wants help*, the smallest man laughs.

Helen and France walking home,
see the men who reel, jeer,
Fucking Arab, at the Sikh.
The men might be drunk,
unspooling another man in the parking lot,
between cars, under an orange sky.
There are no stars above that city.

One swings a baseball bat and
something breaks.

Deliberate, Helen springs
between the men, covers
the shaking figure with herself,
France throws her body over Helen's.

Crushing the man underneath
who whispers over and over, something,
prayer or curse.
They hear the bat against glass.

One of the men kicks France
to kick the man, *tomorrow we'll blast
your fucking country so far your mother will land
in America.*

It is January fourteenth.

⤿

France stands up, takes her weight
off Helen, who trembles, her shoulders
over the man's neck, her arms around
his face, *I'm sorry*, she says.
His ponytail hanging over his forehead,
Where are my glasses?
The long cloth, coiled
around his waist and legs, a limp flag.

The three bend down in the parking lot
search with their fingers.

Shards of windshield glass
blindly reflect the streetlight,
stars in asphalt.

⤿

How melancholy our love-
making. Helen has told me about the man,

about choosing to throw her body
over his. *I acted*, she says.

Now she covers me,
moving above like water, spilling
her arms, neck, shoulders, breasts,
                    the kind of love a wave
has for the shore, the kind of love
that tears away. She believes I
am harder than I am. I am not
steel, not the shores of Hamilton
though I have described
them to her. I am fragile
as sand through the throat
of an hour glass.

France's poem

George Bush is killing butterflies,
he loves them too much —
wants to catch them in his net, but
the net's ring
crushes them into gravel,
smears the parking lot with green
sheen, he wants to know
machinery, how they stutter
through air on sutured wings,
with each swipe
more die at his feet, he does not
weep, he loves them with too much curiosity.

O, I know all about you, sneaky man, your secrets, your
dirty, dirty crime, how you strafed a life boat in World War II
and were never charged, you have been merciless, sickening
quick to denounce atrocities when they were not on your
side, oh you bully, you said Hussein was Hitler but not while
he worked for you, not while you kept him armed, I follow
you, watch you, know your every move, do not think for a
minute I don't hover over you, when he first invaded you
talked oil prices, foreign markets then you decided he was a
moral threat, outraged at his audacity, his *Arab nationalism*,
you had to put him in his place, burn his fort down, little
boys, in '88 you swore never to use food as a tool in foreign
affairs, in '90 you put a food embargo on civilians in Iraq, I
know you, have memorized where you live, lapping cream
from porcelain bowls, know your sneaky mistress who went
unnamed during your term in the White House, I have
touched the bulldog tattoo on your ass, leftovers from your
Princeton fraternity days, I am watching you, violent,
vengeful man, at peace with yourself, I want you at peace
with me, or at least with Schwarzkopf, you called him a *dove*
because he said that *total destruction of Iraq might not be in the
interest of the long-term balance of power in the Middle East*, you
will make sure he doesn't work again, you have tricky ways,
snake, his words don't promote the interest of your friends, I
followed you into the Saudi Sheraton when you visited the
Sabah clan, 234-year monarchs of Kuwait, how easily you
phrased your desire to destroy Iraq, to return their nation to
democracy, your clan has always believed democracy meant
power to the elite, you don't fool me, you refuse to negotiate
because Hussein insists on discussing the Israeli possession
of American nuclear weapons, supposedly illegal by
congressional mandate, about this infraction your so-called
left-wing press has said nothing, O Commander-in-Chief,
you see weapons as the solution, assassin, selling lives for

gold, you want to defeat the anti-weapons bills, to stabilize
the price of gasoline, I know we worry you, though your
press makes the protesters look few and far between,
you should have to pay for the kind of coverage they give
you, but the protesters make you stop and think about costs
to your popularity, and please explain to me why protesters
who opposed the war are *not supporting the troops*, all the ivy
on your diplomas must have taught you that insensibility,
how you fear Arabs, the women's faces, faces you cannot see,
you ask us to hate *Arabs at home*, you go against the UN
decision to use the embargo and have ordered in your
military, but it was your diplomat April Gillespie who told
Hussein days before the invasion that the United States did
not respect the *colonial borders* that established Kuwait, that
you wanted *better and deeper relations* with Iraq — your
crowning achievement will be an Arab nation in flames, your
approval ratings will soar, you are running for re-election
with your flag planted squarely on a hill of civilian bodies,
a dead line of human beings, you and Hussein are grand-
standing, but the price will be a people, cities, and soldiers
exposed to untested weapons, yours are bloody decisions,
but you were head of the CIA, the same CIA that Stockwell
quit when the body of a Central American child was laid
across his desk. Who trained you for this? Was it something
you learned in prep school? And how must I act, my
Captain, O, my captain, to end this chain of chaperoned
brutality?

LAB NOTES
VANCOUVER AQUARIUM

August 1992

I do not believe what they say: no human
corpse shows death by
a human hand until the age of property.

I place the evolution earlier: primates, upright
murder. How human to be cruel. Even in
her body.

Whales returned from land to sea.

Walk on land and be burned
or scorch the earth utterly.

⁓

Though I have flesh
I am inanimate as skeleton
and echo dis-located.

⁓

Night. Wake

It was not a simulation.
Something really happened,
though I did not see it on TV.

Her history sleeps,
buried, I wish to kiss it, awaken
it from   nothing,
                    where she is,
                              a wing,

                                        in thin air.

THE BOMBING

Helen's sky over Baghdad

Like any sky

(except the stars are burning too bright, air
on fire, exploding smart light)

in the television someone says, *More than eighty percent
of the sorties have engaged their targets.*

Everyone wears red, carries gold
engagement rings. It is a wedding,
                                    hands are given
(brides are for burning,
                    a whole constellation burns there).

The American reporter inside Baghdad,
                    We're in the centre of hell.

My sky

Radioactive elements
can be created using alpha particles
to bomb nonradioactive nuclei.
Repulsive forces dominate.

We sit in rows our pencils
jotting notes
no one lifts a head from hush
when a student bursts through the doors,
Baghdad is burning.

She runs beside the lake,
along a path
through snow and concrete.

Between the Hancock Centre and the Prudential
Building she thinks she sees
bombs dropping.
Hears a siren
                    a mother's cry.
The city is burning, citizens burning.

Peering into the sky to see the husk
where blue turns into black —

Impossible to see anything but
Blue, the eggs in the nest.
Turns her face towards
the burning world, New Chicago,
Red, she speaks a fiery language.

Moon and stars hang
billions of miles apart. Parentless.

How righteous death can be.

Imagines her sister
still asleep. They will never share this.

Helen runs in while I'm doing breathing
exercises for diving, *What are you doing, Helen?*
She is deaf

skips into her room, returns.
She throws her arms around me, kisses
my neck, *I do love you*, she says.

Are you rehearsing a melodrama?

I don't see the matches. Are they slipped
into a pocket?
I don't follow her. *Do you hear me?*

I don't take the time.
I am practising, sink back
into breathing.

The last time I see her

Running on the path through
the quadrangles. *Helen*, I call,
waving a hand. She turns.
Does she see me

or see a promise of flames,
                 if she pours oil over her body
will she squeeze through the opening,
find the world she dreams?

Who am I?
Nothing to her.

Spins on her heel.
There's so much to do: gasoline,
more rags, a flame.

Wait. Don't breathe.

❧

What she sees

Through the veil
of her lids, their mother stared hard
at the shapes above her in the cave, then gave
her adult life to find them again,
how they looked at her,
cherishing, tracing her fontanel with promises:
this world will be kind, will lick
your skin, place a golden balm on your forehead.

Helen will fix what has been broken.
She must go back to one tribe, one lamp,
that promising land.

❧

Because what she believed was
big enough for this world — or it was

too small, something anyone
could pack in an overnight bag, strap on
a back, carry at the end of a stick (not even
drooping under the weight), because

it was dangerous, incendiary,
uninspected. Because those who could strike

the match were miles away, boarding
helicopters, hugging wives, sons, daughters,
waving to the crowd (with closed fingers),
were in choppers lifting off from aircraft carriers
(stirring up the brine — the names of the dead
lifting off the waves towards them
in a speech they cannot interpret),

because what she believed crawled
in her belly, rumbling through
the tunnels in her body, shaking her skin
(I put my hand on her wrist
and felt it),
it was not satisfied by rhetoric.

Because it was beautiful
and she fed it.

A painted ibex
in the headlights,
a whale in an ice
sheet, frozen

by her love. Nothing
like her had ever touched me before,
I was in a cavern whose markings I did not recognize.
No recipes.
Colours from a different spectrum.
It was blood inventing channels into new life,
it stung. The way life stings.
The way it hurts to eat when you've been
hungry.

When a despot wants to starve the people
he does not burn their rice, he breaks
their cooking pots.

I came to her without a vessel.

≈

Students thick in the quadrangles,
the sun lecherous
on the white stone buildings, that grey city,
mound of bones, she squats below
the flagpole, dog chain around her neck
and hung from it the sign, *Peace*,
she means this, lifting the heavy metal
canister and bending her neck forward,
as a woman washing her hair will bend
her neck forward, her hair falling over her face

she soaks in gasoline, pours it down her neck,
heavy canister, sloshing gas on her back,
ribbons of gasoline
splash on her jeans, her feet, the snow
on the ground catches it
in pools that rainbow around her, furious
birds overhead, and squirrels, feeding,
oblivious

≈

Helen's poem

My feet are for burning,
are for burning, to send up an SOS.

My back is for burning,
is for burning, a signal flare, a promise.

My face is for sweet burning,
is for sweet burning, my only gift.

And I am for burning, a black candle lit for you.

On fire, dancing. Everyone could see
her eyes, their screaming, someone ran to her
released the rope from the pole
wrapped her electric body
in the flag.

Come into my ship, Love, light the lantern's wick, for I have
trailed too long elsewhere, come Love, I was so near melting
into something, bird, beast, butterfly, threatening to be only
human, Love, I twisted for your taste, waited for you, to feel
you uncurl, flag in me, candle

I want all atoms to open, dust, the silent stretches
between them, unfurl long rows of cables strung, post to
post, the rich fuel of oxygens to burst, mercury flung

Breathe to inhale one another, breathe to eat other lives,
how they build, rumble, stretch, lift the stiff filaments of
their wings, roil into compounds, attached, unattached to
the throng of this body,

The world is too dispersed already, Love, too cyanide,
too bereft, *love is nearer death*

Spooling, nursing on its elements — nitrates, phosphates,
benzene, each ring, my ring — *I live without living myself, and
in such a way I hope, I die because I do not die*

My bones, match sticks, knots of mineral, each envelope,
cell, turned inside out, *arriving in magic, flying, and finally,
insane for the light*, I am Oroboros: searing, raining majestic
ruin, honeying, the velocity of my love for this world.

⤫

Did she reach Baghdad?
Did she, did she, reach it? Give her body?
Did she meet them on the bridge
over the slow river
from New Chicago to the other world,
say, *here I am with you,
I know how burning is?*

⤫

If you burn I will burn too.
I never really believed in life.
I believed only in life, I loved all of you,
I never loved you, I loved only
myself, let me take you into my arms, my house,
my life, *none of these is mine to give, good-bye,*
the earth is home, *death is home,* the earth
is all we have, *no, no, death is what we're working for,*
yes, *no,* I love you, I am you, *I can love*
no one, can never understand you, I am,
I die, I die because your life is worth everything,
your life is worth nothing for I am willing
to give up mine.

LAB NOTES
VANCOUVER AQUARIUM

August 1992

I should have told you —

there are three fundamental laws
of thermodynamics.
You should know the first two.
Energy cannot be created or destroyed.
And the entropy of the universe is always increasing.
There will always be more loss.

⬿

Midnight. Sweating.

I wake into a rage, knowing
you have wasted your life,
frozen yourself in a posture of fury.
Your father's?
You changed nothing, Helen.

Because I loved you enraged, I sculpted this
marble. Now I could smash you to pieces.
Cut out your granite heart or saw
your pray-hand off.

⬿

My sister on the telephone, *Baby bro, Mum is worried about
you. You should go see her or, better, come to Boston — I'll send
you a ticket.*

I can't find a way to speak, words throb my head, a swarm of
mosquitoes with thin black legs, printed on my eyelids like
headlines. *Peter?* she says, *Peter? Ben wants to say hello.*

*Uncle Peter — at Sea Land we saw killer whales like you have in
your aquarium. Do they eat from your hands?*

He has *my* voice:
a telegram from my father's body
through my sister's to Ben —
late news from the vanished.

⁀

I am creature now,
Jew Fish. If nothing is solid
then nothing is simple.
I must rewrite the three laws.

I believed you were all entropy, but no,

Helen, darling, do you see? We have
changed places. The answer, for you,
simple, clear as diamond. A crystal
at absolute zero.

For me, obscuring as a marrow lens.

⁀

A call to her lost father

Will, I have been meaning
to call you, though I hardly know
how to speak back against time —
my voice rattling, a fingered coin dropped
down the glass throat of the token box

giving me entry to the muddied stairs, subway platform —
boarding the mercury train that whirrs
tunnels carved through the fertile soil of a grave world, Will —
I tried to care for her, though I knew her too late
as an astronomer might map the light of a long-dead star,

and I could not keep her: where was I
when she went out?

For what it's worth, I'm done with it.
Because your life's desire for itself sparked
her life, and your death,
her end, because you know how rain
can close into a lover's fist and because
you know its address,
I called to give her back to you,
leaf returned to the branch.

⟳

Postcard to H

Finally I am sick of it.
Tired of your body tenured
between the walls.
An ash house.

I dig a hole
at last. Each mound in the spade
is relief, a deeper breath. I want you

in the ground
outside the
gate. Your own plot. Want you to knock
before you come in. Just that much privacy.

Another grave, wider, farther away.
A room with a shut door.

I have learned to be brutal with the dead.
Expect it of me.

    — P

AFTER HELEN

This morning there are massacres in Kurdistan, Baghdad,
Palestine . . .

In Chicago, a girl
has burned herself in protest.
I want her to be Joan of Arc —
on the pyre, triumphant, dressed in the robes of a monk,
and strong, with the strong legs of a woman.
While she burned, women read the smoke in the sky.
Some refused to spin, others broke
their cooking spoons.
Midwives sifted Joan's smouldering dust into an unguent
to ease the births of difficult children.
This girl, Helen Green, is Joan,
and I am at the chapel in Autun
among pilgrims, walking over stones, lighting
candles where Joan lit them.

This is a dream of solidarity.

Helen Green rests in the last news pages
dumped off the shelves of the magazine stand
and burned in a can
at the corner of 53rd and Avalon
where a ragged woman warms her hands
over Helen's assumption.

Late letter to Helen

We went through the things you left.
Spiral notebooks from class
with notes in the margins —
Coffee 4 o'clock. Medici's.
I'll steal your glasses, kiss
behind your ears —

your closet full of clothes, collection
of baseball caps, passport
(not a single stamp).
Driver's license.
Your patched, faded blue jeans. Poetry.
Will's letter from cummings.
Manon's black and whites,
her teapot, a wall of posters —
I could name your heroes.
There were broken sunglasses,
half-empty bottles of lotion,
shampoo. There were all those things
we wanted to say to you.

Applications and ashtrays. Valentines. Petitions.
Mugs, two souvenir shot glasses. Poems
I wrote for you. The drawing. An address book
filled with names,
a red book filled with sketches, things
you had seen or believed,
as you imagined they might be —
things mostly unfinished.

Sacks and sacks of garbage.
But you are not there, not there.

And how can we be without you?

⌒)

Lost maps

I take the jeans jacket
where it hangs, a vulture, from its hook,
take Helen's jeans from the chest
of drawers, lay them on the bed.
The body remembered, put back

together: neck like a crane,
vivid face (dark eyes, tiny lids), long legs,
bony hips.

In childhood to ease Helen into sleep
France traced around her, skimming
fingers over her sister's edges, Helen squirming,
saying, *it tickles . . . in a good way.*

Later, I was next to her. Ran finger
around her head, flower of ear, down
neck, along arms, bumping over ribs,
finger at her hips, legs, knees, her feet.
Down spine, a rosary, prayer
to the extremities.

> Now I trace Helen's jeans, the smell of
> Helen that slips from seams.
> I hear: *tracer rounds, surgical
> bombing.*

Lost maps, reprise

Her sister takes the jeans jacket
where it hangs from its hook,
takes Helen's jeans from the chest.

What life is there for me to live without her?

Finger down the collar, along arms, bumping over pockets,
finger at legs, knees, the patches.
Zipper. Down seams.
France traces Helen's jeans.

I am lying on the bed, when France
brushes her finger along my face
she begins to trace me
Keep your glasses on, she says.

Together we lie down in darkness.

⌒

2 sisters make love to the same man.

It isn't at the funeral.
It isn't after the body has been
identified.

It happens later, in the silence
that leaks from the death, in the spotlit
search for something unidentified.

That sister wanted her
sister back, bodily, had to become her. And me?
What happens to a man who realizes his lover

desires a whole nation?

⌒

Inside France, breathing
where she came from, holding her
as one holds a body
once one has learned that every body is material.

(What about all those lessons we had: skin
for lampshades, bones for furniture,
whole prisons
built from bodies?
Who learns from history books? Helen gave
better instruction.)

One touches the lover with ceremony,
as though she is already an altar, a boat.

We make love again and again
as if we are scooping the blind eyes
from potatoes nursed in deep graves
or trying to fill these holes.
Something has been left empty.
Unfairly.
Something has been taken.
We were cheated.

Together at night we go looking
in the sore for a poultice.
France tells me the story of their life
as if it were one life.

She has knifed us,
one part of me enraged.
Helen, a terrorist
deaf to all but her own violence —
and if the war was brutal
why choose another brutal act?

•

To the students watching her burn,
to the faculty at the memorial
service, to everyone who wanted an answer,
a hero in a cruel, absurd war,
Helen was magnificent.

And to her lover, her sister,
her foster parents?
More cruel than any war.

•

Days, France falls
into the sky. Over and over
stitching its hem
with silken thread, leaving
needle holes that sting, sewing a great
red robe to cover the lie
of the blue sky.
Blue, she shrieks, furious as she falls,
something has been left in pieces,
something has vanished.
There are no maps any more.

Days, I lie in bed — can't study.
Everything I look at
should tell about her dying.
Everything should be a sign.
I read *Antigone* again, again
only the baldest tragedies make sense.

Sitcom

What if Ismene left at the end with Hymen?
Keep that curtain raised.
What if France and I had a child,
a daughter, and did not name her Helen?
What if we went on to live our lives,
cook our dinners, argue over Friday
nights — how late
the child could stay up, what programs
were acceptable to watch,
and whether the next war was immoral
or not?

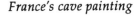

France's cave painting

Spotlights on the library
illuminate its grey hump, pale
as bone. A building that betrays
its structure, columns rise
like ribs to the high roof. Leaded windows
reflect back light, glittering, prismed
insect eyes.

France watches it,
thinking of the dinosaur on the
marbled first floor
of the Museum of Natural History,
a place they visited as children.
She remembers the sign:
Brachiosaurus altithorax
BRAKEeeohSOREos ALteeTHORAX
'arm lizard' with 'deep chest.'
Remembers Helen's O-mouth
as it sounded out the words.

Her arms wrapped around herself,
she presses skin, rising bumps.

Midges gather in the lights. She tilts
her head back, stares.

Knows secrets. Stands in front
of the spotlight beaming up
from the ground. She casts her shadow
over the facade
onto the roof. Bends her back,
arches her arms over her head
towards the ground, spreads her feet apart
like a fluke. She becomes the porpoise —
her distorted shape flung
against the white stone building, swims
alone.

The sea creatures could not breathe
to laugh, they were oil slathered
their bloated corpses buoyed to the surface.

Someone struck a match:

the sea is burning, is burning,
the sea is alight, each molecule flaring
and nothing to douse the fire.

War unwinds at the foot of our bed, between
us. Nothing gives direction.
Underground, prehistoric refineries that churned
ancient peat into oil are burning.
The present coughs up the past
consuming it utterly.
We stare —
the end of the red century.

The soldiers torture the woman's son in front of her.
She had two sons, both dead now,
but only the youngest is tortured
while they hold
her head stiff and force open
her lids.

After that, she loses her sight,
as the curtains will be drawn on a room
where a great crime has happened.
After that, she wakes every morning,
plaits the rugs that will buy her
bread. It is hard to live.

I've done the calculus. Derived the equations.
I don't tell France, asleep beside me —
what I know is too strong —

I know how their crash sent its debris flying
into all our lives. How my father's absence left
me absent to Helen.

But the circles move
beyond those small events, they can't
be held captive.
Holocaust. France
occupied.
The atom bomb, a deadly moon,
pulling history into a tide
of violence, genocides
of this half-century dragged in its wake.

These events are not just beads on a rosary,
vertebrae on a spine,
secret tunnels
run between them:
catacombs beneath
a mirrored city.

Cave walls lie.
A skeleton grows inside us
(a swallowed seed sprouts a smoke tree)
mineral by mineral
from the world we breathe, toxic lakes, from molecules
themselves, or bomb-laced atoms, countless
half-lives,
each nucleus a cradle for cruelty.

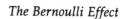

The Bernoulli Effect

I can't bear silent lovemaking.
As if France's language were just for Helen.

I tell her about the Bernoulli Effect.
How it can make a ship sail
into wind, how it lifts an airplane wing.

The wing splits the air that rushes
headlong across it. High pressure below.
Low pressure above.
Barrelling backwards, towards union.

A kind of madness, France weeps,
thank you for that.

For what? I ask, immune.

France's song

Once there was a girl who gave herself
to the Virgin, built herself behind stones
into crumbling church walls. Anchoress,
she was fed through a thin opening,
passed out her piss, her shit.
People came to her for prophecies:
who would give birth, which fields to sow.
The girl saw pictures of animals,
grains, she saw gold threads, words in red.

My sister loved the world too much
and passed me her waste.

I could bury myself inside her cave,
rush, a mad atom, towards her,
live the rest of my life trying to rebuild
her body or cover her grave.

Instead I drop —
marry myself to myself.

Emptiness echoing.

Go back to the *bluest blue*, find
love in sky-lake, again, again.

⤙

Torches of fish
move around the cumbersome
lunged beast in her thick suit fitted with
a microphone. As she speaks
bubbles of words rise between darting fish
towards the still surface.
Her voice, naming those who eat from her hands,
travels unfathomable distances
to arrive at the dusty speaker's mouth
mounted in a corner.

France watches her, longing for
peace in an atmosphere with false
air. I watch her as though watching
something beamed towards me reassemble
in particles of light. I look at France
the same way.

There is nothing to say.

⤙

A visit from Helen

All morning it throws itself against glass,
again, again,
picks itself up from the floor
where it lies, concussed, jumps
to its feet, lifts off.
Something is beyond the glass, in the green
outside. Something half-seen.
Like the atom hurtling
through gold foil, it
will find the opening.

Perhaps she knows we are, after all, wholly air.

I hear its repeated
silence in the room
where light filters through stained
glass. Hardening.
When I arrive, it is dead

for a moment, then
awake in my hand; neck
straight, wings unfolded.

In August I flew
to Vancouver. France flew
elsewhere.
A thousand names —
roads, rivers, mountains,
borders, fault lines —
separate us.

The grass grew over Baghdad,
as it has grown back over
the globe's skull,
again, again,

and the soil was rich
with hemoglobin

Bechtel Corporation
contracted to
articulate the city again,

if you want
the citizens, they are
blades,

Above their graves
night leans down its shattered
forehead.

EPILOGUE

Last night I dreamt the red book. A glow, a tongue dipped in uranium, the torch-tail of a firefly. Touch its pages — they ignite.

The book was a Siamese painting, herds lost on vessels sailing dry rivers. There were drawings on its pages that came alive as if traced onto paper with tints of living cells.

A village without walls. I saw her there, with the others — her father, her mother, the familiar dead. I did not speak to Will — I saw my own face as if in the shadow cast by a mirror. I looked again to know it was my father, a tag round his neck like a chain, Private Peter Hull. So beautiful it flushed me with desire.

The faces of the beloved dead, petals of a flower, mouth agape, sick for rain, air, for enough soil to make a grave.

I understood then that I could slip between bone signatures bound to the book's spine. Such temptation — to become the anchorite. But I could not enter there and live.

Close the book, now feathers, light as ash.

For the first time — a cry, as if an orca pod were translating the meaning of its sounds, a round, each verse overlapping the other, green song circling, a wreath cast into watery sleep. Reason married to imagination. Benzene ring.

For a moment, below the surface, I find oxygen in water — against the loss, I sing myself awake.

— Peter Hull, August 12, 1992

NOTES

On February 16, 1991, Gregory Levey burned himself to death to protest the Persian Gulf War. I hope this poem helps to preserve his name and his action in the Red Book — now estimated to be half a million names long — that lists those deaths caused directly or indirectly by the Persian Gulf War. I did not know Gregory Levey, nor do I claim to understand why he killed himself. The characters in this poem are entirely fictitious.

•

Page 49: drawing of the whale in ice is by Stephen Quick.
Page 51: line in italics is Peter's misquoting of a line from H. D.'s poem "The Walls Do Not Fall."
Pages 75–76: in "They infect her dreams," lines in italics are from CNN broadcasts of the Persian Gulf War. The statistic given by the Pentagon that suggested that "80% of the bombs engaged their targets" was fallacious, the result of "perception management" on the part of the army. In fact, the much lauded weapons of the American army were, according to a report published four years after the war, about 20% accurate. This number was overlooked in the congressional decisions to continue stockpiling these weapons.
Page 95: Helen's poem — After a poem by Osip Mandelstam; the last line is his.
Page 96: Helen's song — First quotation from St. Teresa de Avila. Second quotation from Goethe's "The Holy Longing" a poem to which this poem is indebted.
Page 107: this poem is adapted from the author's poem, "Leaving the Fundamental Assumptions Unexpressed," published in *Carrying Place* (House of Anansi Press, 1995).
Page 108: line in italics is from "Epitaph" by Marina Tsvetaeva.

Page 109: first line in italics is spoken by Ismene in Sophocles' *Antigone*.
Page 115: line in italics is from Tim Lilburn's *Moosewood Sandhills*.
Page 120: lines in italics are by Georg Trakl.
Epilogue — For the red book I am indebted to the poet Li-Young Lee.

Every reasonable effort has been made to contact the holders of copyright for materials quoted in this work. The author and the publisher will gladly receive information that will enable them to rectify any inadvertent errors or omissions in subsequent editions.

ACKNOWLEDGEMENTS

Thanks to the Ontario Arts Council and to the Sage Hill Experience. Many thanks to my editor, Don McKay, who guided the book into print with kind hands.

Some poems were published in a different form in *Carousel*, *Grain*, and *This Magazine*. My thanks to the editors of those publications, especially Kevin Connolly and Daniel Evans.

I would like to acknowledge the inspiration provided by the following texts and recordings: Peter Dale Scott's *Coming to Jakarta*; Noam Chomsky's taped lectures, including *On U.S. Gulf Policy*; Li-Young Lee's *The City in Which I Love You* and *Rose*; Carolyn Forché's anthology *Against Forgetting* and her book *The Angel of History*; *Z Magazine*; Joni Mitchell's *Blue*; The Cowboy Junkies' *Trinity Sessions*; Tim Lilburn's *Moosewood Sandhills*; Michael Redhill's *Lake Nora Arms*; Yeats' *Crazy Jane Poems*; Sophocles' *Antigone*; C. K. Williams' *A Dream of Mind*; Anthony Minghella's *Cigarettes and Chocolate*; John Berger's *To the Wedding*; Steven Heighton's *The Ecstasy of Skeptics*; and Osip Mandelstam's *Selected Poems*.

My love and gratitude to Lou and Laura Bernieri, who saw me through 1991. Much love and thanks to my mother (who can sing through anything), to Michael, and to my grandmothers.

For their generous comments, their guidance, and friendship I am indebted to Janice Kulyk Keefer, Constance Rooke, and Martha Sharpe at Anansi, and to Jane Bohman, Gillian Deacon, Louise B. Halfe, Tim Lilburn, Pamela Kaczanowski, Susan Kernohan, Elizabeth McHenry, Michael Redhill, Mansel Robinson, Patricia Seaman, and Julia Wenniger. And thanks to the artist Stephen Quick, and to those at the Shoals Marine Laboratory, especially J. B. Heiser, Chris Bogdanowicz, and the skeletal minke, Elly. I am grateful to Kristin Spalding, *tendrilly*, for the anchorites and to d—, *north star*.